NOTTINGHAMSHIRE
AT WORK

Casks being opened at John Player & Sons to reveal the raw material prior to being turned into cigarettes.

BRITAIN IN OLD PHOTOGRAPHS

NOTTINGHAMSHIRE AT WORK

DAVID J. OTTEWELL

SUTTON PUBLISHING LIMITED

Sutton Publishing Limited
Phoenix Mill · Thrupp · Stroud
Gloucestershire · GL5 2BU

First published 1996

Title page photograph: Wilson's Windmill,
Retford, *c.* 1905.

British Library Cataloguing in Publication Data
A catalogue record for this book is available from the
British Library.

ISBN 0-7509-1278-2

Typeset in 10/12 Perpetua.
Typesetting and origination by
Sutton Publishing Limited.
Printed in Great Britain by
Ebenezer Baylis, Worcester.

CONTENTS

Early production at Raleigh Cycle Co.

INTRODUCTION

Although a picturesque county, containing as it does Sherwood Forest and the Dukeries to the north and running into the Vale of Belvoir in the south, Nottinghamshire is also a world-renowned industrial centre. Its situation in the heart of England, well served by roads, railways and waterways, has contributed to Nottinghamshire's industrial success as has the availability of ready sources of power and a plentiful, skilled and willing workforce.

Nottinghamshire has been blessed with huge coal reserves. Although this traditional industry is now sadly in decline, for over a century it has supplied a cheap and abundant source of power and fuel both for domestic use and more importantly for manufacturing industry.

Nottinghamshire has a deservedly worldwide reputation for the quality of its lace. The Leavers lace machine which revolutionized patterned lace making was invented in the town. In the nineteenth and early twentieth century people came from far and wide to visit the Lace Market area of Nottingham.

The hosiery trade has a long and turbulent history in Nottingham. Many people scratched a living from it in the eighteenth and nineteenth centuries and there was a great deal of poverty and exploitation, including the shipping in of children from London to work in grim, dangerous conditions. William Lee, a curate in the Nottinghamshire village of Calverton, invented a stocking machine. However, not all new developments were welcomed and the Luddites were active in the town. Today some of the most innovative and best made clothes are manufactured in Nottinghamshire.

From quite unpromising beginnings three Victorian men based in Nottingham fought their way up to head nationally recognized companies. In the cases of John Player and Jesse Boot, with little money behind them they built up companies so that their names became synonymous with their business ventures. Like the third member of the triumvirate, Frank Bowden, developer of Raleigh Bicycles, they had an eye for the market and the skill to produce what people wanted.

A great deal of Nottinghamshire's industrial success has been based on its diversity: not for her, dependence on one main industry with decline occurring if that industry faltered; rather, a range of manufacturing from telecommunications to tins, soap to foodstuffs. Similarly, its natural resources have not just been based on coal; oil, gypsum and gravel have been successfully extracted and sold.

The requirements of local people should not be forgotten. Although a manufacturing centre, Nottinghamshire has a lot of farmland providing work for many and food for countless more.

A host of service industries from skilled doctors and nurses to delivery drivers, waitresses and shop workers provide work for many thousands of people who make a vital contribution to daily life.

Both its enviable geographical situation and setting and its manufacturing skills have contributed to make Nottinghamshire truly the 'Queen of the Midlands', a title it proudly boasts.

NOTTINGHAM LACE

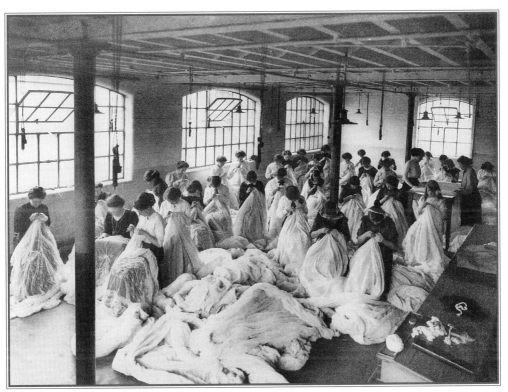

Nottingham is world famous for the quality of its lace. Birkin and Co., founded in 1827 by Richard Birkin and based at Gladstone Street, Basford, is one of the premier companies. The women here are concentrating on the fiddly job of mending lace. Note the large windows that provide as much natural light as possible.

The Lace Market area of Nottingham, situated around St Mary's Church. The Lace Market consisted of a series of narrow streets flanked by tall lace factories and offices. Each day the streets would be thronged with workers arriving and departing. The buildings were designed to impress visitors. Birkin and Co. had a warehouse here on Broadway.

A view inside Thomas Adams' Talbot Street lace curtain factory. This room of heavy machines helped to produce between 1,000 and 1,200 pairs of curtains each week. Its nationwide reputation is demonstrated by the fact that King George V and Queen Mary paid a visit on Wednesday 24 June 1914.

Lace making, 1914. It is interesting to see that it is the men who are in charge of the heavy Leavers' lace machines, which could produce large quantities of fancy lace.

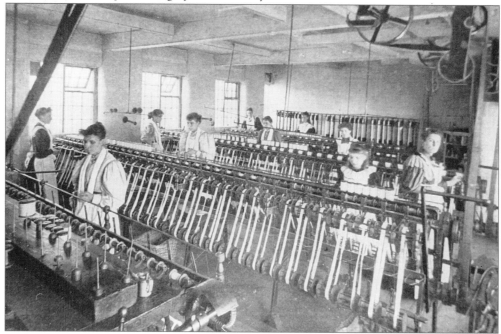

Birkin and Co. had their factory in New Basford. These ladies are working in the winding room. A few employees could supervise a number of machines.

The main dressing room in the Adams' factory. The picture gives an idea of its dimensions: 110 yards long and 265 yards wide. Here the lace was stretched after initial processing.

St Ann's Well Road was the site of the Midland Lace Company. This photograph dates from 1906. Again large windows provide an abundance of natural light to help the women see the intricate patterns on the lace.

Thomas Adams Ltd. The various vats contained different dyes providing colours for the lace. Again this area appears to be basically a male preserve.

Another area of the Adams' lace factory involved in processing was the bleaching house, where huge lengths of lace were given a pristine white finish.

Another view in Birkin and Co., 1905. This picture shows a large number of women, many apparently quite young, in the clipping room. Concentration was the key to producing quality lacework. The women are carefully removing loose threads without damaging the intricate lace patterns.

This 1915 postcard uses an example of locally produced lace to frame a group of menders busy at their task. Although machines were involved in the manufacturing process, there was still a great deal of work to be done by hand where skilled and nimble fingers were essential.

These ladies are busily working in the so-called 'brown room'. It was here that the lace was taken after removal from the machine so that it could be arranged for bleaching and sorted before it was dyed.

An Edwardian postcard showing a group of lace jenniers and finishers at work in an unknown factory in Nottingham. There were a number of factories in the area where similar processes were undertaken.

The finishing department, where the beautiful end product reached the end of the production process, with final mending, cutting up, scalloping and knitting.

A clever use of a Nottingham lace border to decorate an Edwardian postcard showing a pair of local churches. The intricate designs made by machine often resulted in slight breaks which had to be mended by hand.

BOOTS PURE DRUG CO.

In 1891 Jesse Boot obtained the lease on a shop on the corner of Pelham Street and High Street, Nottingham. The new shop incorporated all his latest retail ideas, which he tried out here before installing them in his other branches.

The Island Street laboratories. When Jesse Boot found his original Goose Gate premises overcrowded he moved his wholesale and manufacturing enterprises to the Island Street area of Nottingham, creating employment for many people. The waterway in the foreground provided a source of transport for both the raw materials and the finished articles, as did the nearby railway.

Tablet machine room. Millions of tablets were manufactured each working day to supply the ever-expanding Boots chain of shops.

Tablet department packing room. The packing of the manufactured tablets was a major undertaking and a large, mainly female, workforce was kept very busy in this department. Note the caps and overalls worn to maintain hygiene standards.

Technical research laboratory. Much of Jesse Boot's success was based on the introduction of new lines. Technical research was therefore very important to the company.

Plaisaunce, West Bridgford. Jesse Boot and his wife had the utmost regard for the care and welfare of their employees and often invited groups of them down to their summer house. Plaisaunce was built on the banks of the River Trent.

Mrs. Jesse Boot

requests the pleasure of

Miss Clay's

Company at a Garden Party, "Plaisaunce,"

Wilford Lane, on Saturday, July 28th,

3 to 9 o'clock.

A typical invitation to a Boots employee from Mrs Jesse Boot. By the river employees could relax or engage in tennis and other sports.

When his central Nottingham site proved too small, Jesse Boot planned to develop a vast site at Beeston on the outskirts of the city. He was heavily involved in building the new university at Highfields, so his son John was the leading light in the new factory development.

D10 building, Beeston. Designed by Sir Owen Williams, D10 was opened in July 1933 and has won awards for its architecture. Unfortunately Sir Jesse Boot died before he could see his new landmark building.

A selection of Boots transport with a Foden's 'box-type' steam lorry to the centre of the picture. These were needed to transport the finished products to shops in an ever-widening area.

Pastille manufacture, *c*. 1955. These ladies, hygienically attired in overalls, caps and gloves, are involved in drying pastilles after glazing.

Pastille manufacture in D6. Careful work and inspection at all stages were the key elements in the production of top quality products.

The packing hall, D6, *c.* 1963. Boots has always been very careful about the cleanliness of its factory departments.

JOHN PLAYER & SONS

An aerial view showing the John Player & Sons tobacco factory in the Radford area of Nottingham. To the front is Factory no. 1 with Factory no. 2, which was completed in 1932, situated behind it. The presence of Players in Nottingham has been very important to the economy of the city.

John Player & Sons offices. These buildings fronted on to Radford Boulevard. By 1926 Player's employed over 5,000 staff and therefore needed an extensive administration and sales structure.

A group of women involved in handwork on the tobacco: a very labour-intensive operation, with only small amounts of tobacco being worked on at a time.

In 1932 Player's produced this superb advert for their Medium Navy Cut cigarettes, which they state were made 'in this sunny modern factory'.

This austere building is John Player & Sons bonded warehouse situated on Ilkeston Road. The loading bay can be seen linking the two tall buildings.

Here we see two factory workers at work opening a huge pack of tobacco, *c.* 1930. The casks were known as tierces and after opening the leaf was weighed before being processed.

The overall-clad ladies are sitting at their machines stemming the tobacco. Most of the stems were removed by machine but some had to be done by hand.

Much of the tobacco for making cigarettes was moved from section to section by machine. This machine is taking the stemless tobacco on its way to a rotary conditioning machine.

Even in the 1930s Player's used sophisticated machinery in the manufacture of cigarettes. This machine is cutting the tobacco, with the man at the rear feeding in the uncut version and the man at the front extracting the small uniform strands.

Female employees standing at machines making 'Medium Navy Cut' cigarettes, probably 1940s. The tobacco is being put into cigarette paper and then shaped, sealed and cut.

These two young Player's workers are engaged in the process known as tucking in outers – preparing cartons to receive the finished cigarettes.

Lorries no. 2 and no. 7 in the Player's fleet. They would have been a familiar sight around the streets of Lenton and Radford in the inter-war years.

No. 1 Factory. This large room stretching into the distance, with women standing at benches, was known as the box department.

This aerial view shows Churchfield Lane in Radford, where Player's manufactured cases to hold their tobacco products, 1930s.

An impressive line-up of Player's delivery vans, 1925. The men appear to have dressed up especially for the occasion. The Player's trade mark can be seen on the side of the second van from the right.

This gallant band is the John Player & Sons fire brigade, always on hand to tackle any emergency within the factory complex. Many are proudly sporting medals.

The John Player & Sons offices were patriotically decorated for the arrival of the King and Queen on 24 June 1914.

RALEIGH INDUSTRIES

The Raleigh Industries Ltd head office on Lenton Boulevard. Note the impressive relief friezes all along the frontage between the ground floor and first floor windows. In 1896 production was transferred from Raleigh Street to a 7½-acre site on Faraday Road, where 850 people were employed.

This unprepossessing doorway on Raleigh
Street led to the workshop from which the
famous Raleigh Company grew.

A view of the interior of the press shop at Raleigh, during the early years of this century. The bins to the
front contain a selection of parts ready for production.

Early days at Raleigh: a workshop with bicycles in various stages of construction. The men are all in hats and the ladies in long black dresses.

An aerial photograph showing the extensive Raleigh Cycle Co. factory in the Lenton area, 1930s. Many of the nearby houses were homes for the workers. By 1939 Raleigh was producing 400,000 bikes per year, which was to rise to 1½ million by 1960.

Five to four in the afternoon, and the men in the drawing office are hard at work. Development of new products was a key feature of the expanding company.

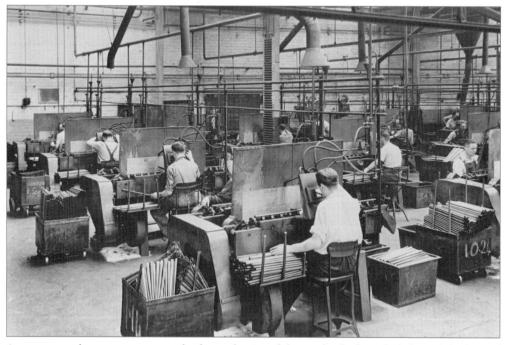

A monotonous but very necessary task: the production of thousands of tubes which formed the basis of the bicycle assembly.

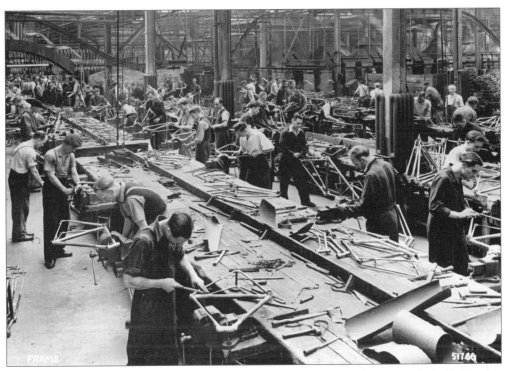

The tubes made in the previous picture went towards making the bicycle frame, to which all the other components were then added.

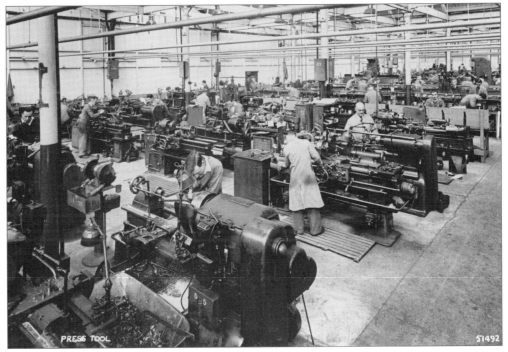

The heavy machines turning out precision parts in the press tool section. Compared with the picture on page 44 we can see the development of the manufacturing machines in use.

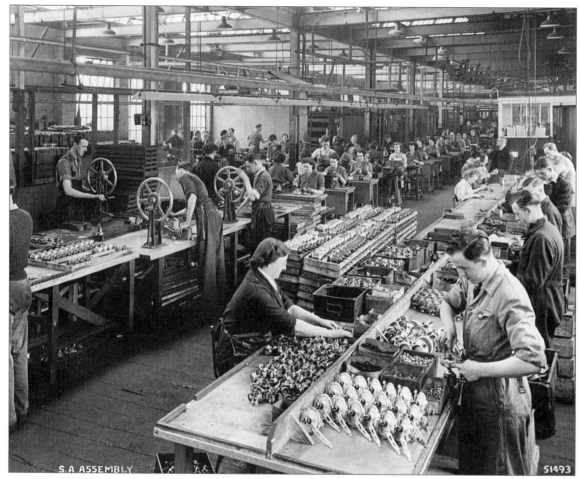

A hive of activity in the Sturmey Archer gears assembly section of the factory. The specialist area of production was one of the keys to Raleigh's success. By 1960 it was turning out 2 million Sturmey Archer units a year.

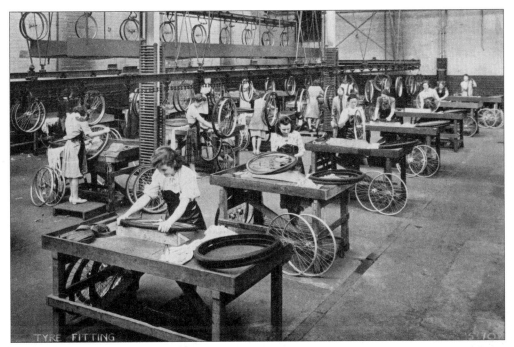

The tyre fitting department, which at the time of this picture at least appears to have been a female preserve.

A busy assembly shop where men and women work side by side to produce a superior product, here reaching the end of its manufacturing process, 1955.

An employee in the later stages of assembling a child's Chopper cycle, all the rage in the 1970s. Raleigh has prided itself on producing new items for an increasingly sophisticated market.

The busy production line at Raleigh, 1955. These sturdily built bikes are almost at the finished stage. I remember seeing many employees travelling to and from work on similar machines. The overhead conveyor system is moving each bike from one area to another.

After a busy morning's work the huge canteen would soon be crowded with employees. Some brought their own 'snap' while others were supplied from the Raleigh kitchens.

Raleigh did not only produce bicycles. Here are some toys for younger children to ride on being assembled. The same detailed work went into toys as was given to the bicycles.

THE COAL INDUSTRY

Newstead Colliery no. 1 rescue team. Coal mining was, and still is, a dangerous occupation. Each colliery had its own fully trained and equipped rescue team on call for any emergency. They are wearing the latest breathing apparatus. Gas was a frequent danger underground.

A primitive colliery. The Victorian Kimberley Colliery was situated in the Swingate area. It opened in 1852, closing in 1897. It is hard to imagine the appalling conditions the men worked in or the risks they took.

Mansfield Colliery, Forest Town. Mining played a big part in many people's lives around Mansfield. The Bolsover Colliery Company sank this pit in 1903 and extracted the first coal in July 1909. Conditions were bleak and its pit-head baths were not opened until May 1936.

A trio of miners still in their pit dirt. For many years mineworkers had to cope without pit-head baths, and indeed in most cases without bathrooms at home. Note the Davy safety lamps, vital equipment.

Scratching for coal, East Kirkby, 1912. During the strike of 1912 miners had to resort to digging on spoil heaps and open-casting in order to keep body and soul together.

Brinsley Colliery. Often men had to work in very cramped and uncomfortable conditions as this miner, hewing coal with a pick, illustrates.

Clifton Colliery: underground at the meeting of two roadways. A loaded truck is emerging from one side while an empty one is just returning.

Brinsley Colliery, Eastwood. A turn-of-the-century view underground showing a pair of miners with a pit pony, which is pulling a loaded tub. The lamps carried by the miners were ever present but the safety helmet of today is not in evidence.

Clifton Colliery. The coal face is often many hundreds of feet underground. These men are ascending in the cage after a punishing shift.

H.L.MOREL NOTTINGHAM.

Clifton Colliery: the end of a shift and the men are leaving the pit top. Note how all the men are in cloth caps. To the front are a pair of upturned pit trucks.

Clifton Colliery, *c.* 1895. Young children might have been stopped from descending the shafts by this stage of the nineteenth century, but some of these boys picking coal in the screens at Clifton seem very young.

A gathering at the pit top, Clifton Colliery, 1926. Three pit ponies, their eyes blinkered with leather masks, take in the fresh air. The presence of the policeman in uniform and the date tend to suggest that this was at the time of the General Strike.

Harworth Colliery, a very sophisticated pit for its time. Originally sunk by a German company just before the First World War, Harworth soon came under the control of the Barber Walker Company of Eastwood.

Cotgrave Colliery first produced coal as recently as 1964. Staffed largely with miners transferred from Scotland and the north-east, the pit only had a short life: production ceased in October 1992.

Teversal Colliery pit-head. In Victorian and Edwardian times miners undertook some terrific feats of engineering, usually out of sight of most people. Here they have combined to build a pyramid of sleepers and pit props probably as a base for a bonfire to celebrate the coronation of King George V in June 1911.

Bestwood Coal and Iron Company's works opened in 1874. When in full production four blast furnaces were in operation. Iron making came to an end in the 1920s.

Drilling for oil at Eakring. Britain's first commercial on shore oilfield was discovered by D'Arcy Exploration in Nottinghamshire in 1939. It made a significant contribution to the war effort and continued to produce until 1965. A selection of 'nodding donkeys' remain in Duke's Wood, Eakring today.

MANUFACTURING

A group of local carpenters taking time out from their work to pose for the photographer in the middle of the main street through Kimberley.

These framework knitters' houses were situated on Normanton Street and Taylor Street in Broad Marsh. They are interesting because of the 'top shops' built on the roofs to provide as much natural light as possible for the home workers.

Framework knitters' workshops. These premises are on Poplar Street. Parliament Street again had large windows on the upper floors to admit natural light to aid working.

The first cotton mill in the world. James Hargreaves, the inventor of the spinning jenny which mechanized the manufacture of cotton, was driven out of his native Blackburn and fled to Nottingham, where in 1767 he opened a small cotton mill just off Wollaton Street.

A group of female hosiery workers at the turn of the century. They were employed by Vann and Co.

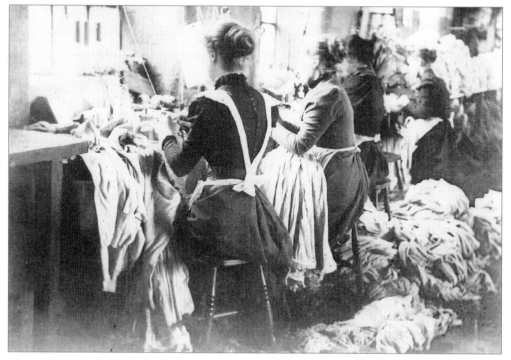

The same workers back at their benches. Vann and Co. hosiery manufacturers had premises at 6 Greyfriar Gate and Alfred Street Mills, Ashforth Street.

Hosiery manufacturers I. and R. Morley: a room of underwear-making machines at their Manvers Street factory, 1924. Nottingham was the centre of the British hosiery industry and many developments of hosiery machines were made in the town.

Bairnswear Ltd was a well-known clothing manufacturer in the Basford area of Nottingham for a number of years, providing employment for many workers.

Hollins Mill, Radford. The Nottingham area is littered with a number of hosiery mills. This one is typical of many, presenting a large and impressive exterior to potential customers.

Field Mill, Mansfield. Although many of the mills are centred on Nottingham and its suburbs others did exist. Mansfield had a number including Field Mill, built in the eighteenth century by the Duke of Portland. It was driven by power from a 40 ft diameter water wheel.

This extensive factory belonging to Aristoc Limited was situated on the Nottinghamshire–Derbyshire border at Langley Mill. Developed from the family firm of A.E. Allen and Co., this was a stocking manufacturer. In the 1960s the company claimed to use over 100,000 miles of nylon yarn each day.

Established in 1756, the Compressed Leather Company Ltd's factory at Giltbrook had an imposing tower. A number of the female members of the workforce can be seen assembled by the front entrance, taking time off from their work manufacturing parts for shoes.

The Campion Cycle Company Ltd, 1904. When this picture of the assembly shop was taken the company had premises at 2–4 Carlton Street and on Liverpool Street. There were many cycle companies in the Nottingham area meeting the needs of a popular hobby.

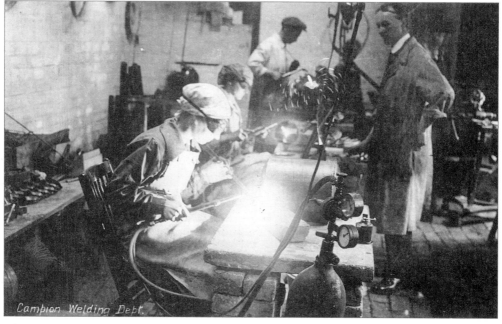

Like many other companies, Campion Cycles helped the national effort during the First World War. Here, in 1917, the factory has been given over to producing aircraft parts. Mr Henry Campion himself is standing supervising welding work.

Cigar manufacturers E. Alton operated from a factory of some size at the junction of Derby Road and Ilkeston Road. They had a good reputation for the quality of their product. This postcard view dates from 1924.

F. Chambers Garden Pencil Works and Kenya Works, situated in Stapleford. They used cedar wood to manufacture pencils and crayons. On this advertising card they claimed 'The factories are equipped with the latest automatic machinery and labour saving devices.'

A pair of workers in Moore's Dairy checking on a glass-lined milk pasteuriser tank. The company claimed: 'Try our bottled milk and note the rich cream line.'

Moore and Sons' Dairy was situated at 119 Burford Road, Hyson Green. This picture shows part of the milk cooling and bottling apparatus.

The Nottingham firm of Gunn and Moore is known worldwide in cricket playing countries for the quality of its cricket bats. Inside the Castle Boulevard factory we see bats in various stages of production. Many international cricketers can still be seen today wielding Gunn and Moore bats.

Beeston Humber Works, 1907. Thomas Humber started his cycle works in 1880 and soon employed 1,800 people. He began experimenting with motor car building, and when by 1908 this proved profitable he moved his premises and many of his workers to Coventry.

Ericsson's Telephone Works, Beeston. Established in 1903, Ericsson's was a subsidiary of a Swedish company. By 1967 its original workforce of 130 had grown to over 8,000.

An operative engaged in adjusting telephone dials, Ericsson's Telephones Ltd. A fair degree of manual dexterity was required for such precision work. As the presence of telephones increased in households so did the prosperity of Ericsson's, and the scale of their operations.

A section of the vast Plessey Telecommunications operation. Here the workers are putting Reed relays together for use in Plessey 'Pentex' electronic exchanges.

Operations at Plessey, Beeston, where we see an electronic unit assembly line, 1960s. The components are worked on before being returned to the conveyor belt.

Plessey, probably early 1960s. A group of workers engaged on telephone assembly is using the flow line (conveyor belt) method.

Plessey. The board at the front encourages employees to achieve production targets. They are using gun wrapping techniques on terminating crossbar switch wiring.

Kiddier's Brushmakers, 1902. This is the dingy interior of William Kiddier's factory at 23–5 Sneinton Street. The various brushes made here were sold from a shop on South Parade.

Hardy's Brewery, Kimberley. The brewery at Kimberley was built in 1861. It is said the site was chosen for its supply of pure water. Thirty years later another company, Hansons, built a brewery close by. Eventually, in October 1930, the two amalgamated to form the famous Hardy and Hanson's Brewery.

This long, low-ceilinged building is Shipstone's Maltings, which was situated on Eland Street, Basford. James Shipstone and Sons Ltd, a famous Nottingham brewery, was founded in 1852.

Shipstone's Brewery, Basford. The wearing of wellingtons and plastic aprons shows the wet and messy nature of some of the tasks involved in brewing beer.

Shipstone's Brewery. The three workers are seen here whipping down a yeast head in a large tank. The beer was brewed in large quantities before being put into casks.

Coopering is a very skilled trade and an essential component of the work at Shipstone's Brewery. The need for coopers is drastically reduced today, as modern metal casks are widely used.

RURAL OCCUPATIONS

THE SMITHY, CROPWELL BUTLER (NO. 2).

COPYRIGHT, J.S. & S.

The smithy at Cropwell Butler, c. 1916. This view illustrates both the old and new: the farrier is hard at work on his traditional craft, but his smithy is about to be passed by a car. These would ultimately make many blacksmiths obsolete.

The horse was an important part of farming life. This colt, pictured on a postcard advertising Makbar meal and cake nuggets, belonged to H. Breedon of Car Colston. He won First Prize at the Flintham Show on 16 October 1913.

Gonalston smithy, 1912. The smithy was an essential part of country life. The giant horseshoe in brick on the front of the building is quite traditional. Other examples in Nottinghamshire are at Plumtree and Carlton on Trent.

The horseshoe pile at Scarrington: a tangible way of seeing how much shoeing George Flinders, the blacksmith, undertook between 1945 and 1965. The pile is 17 ft tall and measures 19ft 6in round its base. It is estimated to contain 50,000 horseshoes.

Out in the fields. Nottinghamshire has a lot of farmland. In days gone by the true meaning of horsepower really applied. Today machinery has removed much of the back-breaking and slow work previously associated with agriculture.

Clifton Green near Nottingham. The farmer is making his way from the fields. His horse is pulling a fully laden haycart back to the barn.

Loading bracken near Mansfield, 1916. Many of the tasks in the countryside were labour intensive. Here a dozen men are involved in the task of cutting and clearing bracken just from a small area of woodland.

Wiseton cricket field. In times of shortage you make do with what's available. These German prisoners of war were set to renovating the cricket field in front of Wiseton Hall — surely a preferable pursuit to taking part in a war.

The windmill at Sutton-in-Ashfield was built by William Downing Adlington of Park House, Skegby, in about 1810. The bridge at Sutton Junction station can be seen in the background of this 1907 photograph. In 1917 the mill was destroyed in a fire.

Moore's Mill, Laneham, 1910. Like many windmills it served the needs of farmers in the local community. This view shows its rural setting.

The mill at Caythorpe, *c.* 1910. Wind power was not always reliable or indeed available. Water mills, such as this impressive one at Caythorpe, provided an alternative place for the farmers to take their wheat and corn.

Sinking for New Well. Burton Joyce Pumbing Station

These workmen were sinking a new well for a pumping station at Burton Joyce, 1909. The search for local sources of water was quite keen, as the alternative was piping it in from long distances. This view was taken by local man J.H. Scott of Bulcote.

E. Gaudwell had their large mill buildings by the River Greet in Southwell. As this advertising card proudly states, they were the winners of the Nottinghamshire Bakers Cup three years running from 1907 to 1909. Today the mill is being turned into apartments.

Sutton-in-Ashfield bone mill. Mills were not only for the processing of wheat and corn. This one at Sutton was involved in grinding down animal remains. Unfortunately, as can be seen, it was ravaged by fire.

Thomas Richmond and Son of Newark manufactured churns and other equipment for the farming community. Here is their stall at the Newark Show, with a hand-operated butter churn to the fore. Richmonds had a shop, The Cooperage, at 4 Boar Lane in Newark.

Fiskerton Dairy School class. H. Barrett of Southwell took this photograph on 16 April 1911. It shows a group of ladies who were attending classes at the Midland Agricultural Dairy College travelling dairy school. Possibly they would go on to use the butter churn being sold above.

DELIVERY VEHICLES

R. Blount, the baker, operated from premises at 79 Birkin Avenue, Hyson Green. His impressive delivery horse and cart is seen here parked in Nottingham Cattle Market. It was quite a familiar sight to see merchants delivering their goods in this fashion before horses and carts were superseded by motorized vehicles after the First World War.

An Edwardian view of the mail cart outside the post office at Burton Joyce. This would be the last collection of the day, at 7 p.m., after which the mail would be taken to Nottingham for sorting. Nearly every village had its own post office at this time so there were a number of mail-carts touring the outlying villages to collect and deliver mail.

At the end of the last century farmer C. Gunn of Manor Farm, Vicarage Lane, Ruddington, used this horse and trap to transport himself and small loads around the district.

Bread delivery in Woodborough, 1916. W.P. Henshaw has travelled from his hygienic bakery in Lambley to deliver corn and flour and wheatmeal as well as bread to the nearby village of Woodborough. Here he is parked outside the village shop.

Lamp oil deliveries in Walkeringham, 1907. Before the spread of electricity and gas supplies to outlying villages people had to rely on oil lamps. Horse-drawn carts with tanks mounted on them would travel from village to village delivering supplies. This cart contains 'White Rose Finest American Lamp Oil'.

Butcher's cart in Hickling, 1907. The lack of individual family transport in the early years of this century meant that many outlying villages relied on travelling merchants to supply many of their needs.

With a few notable exceptions we rarely encounter a toll keeper today, but in the past they were a more common sight. This toll house near Sutton-in-Ashfield was photographed in 1872. Mrs Shore, seated with the baby, collected 1½d for a horse and 3d for a horse and cart.

Monarch Transport, Nottingham. This early lorry with its solid tyres must have given a rough ride. The baskets from hosiery manufacturers, I. and R. Morley, would have made a very unstable load, especially as many of the roads were far from smooth.

Henry Ashwell and Co. Ltd, based in Basford, used this lorry to transport cloth after they had put it through finishing processes such as mercerizing (giving cotton a lustre), dyeing or bleaching. This picture is slightly more recent than the one above: the lorry has pneumatic tyres.

A group of employees from L. Block and Company, Middle Pavement, seen here with their delivery vehicles outside the gates of Wollaton Park on Middleton Boulevard, Nottingham, 1950s.

L. Block and Co. dealt with Kelvinator refrigerators, and here one is being demonstrated. The bottle crates in the background are from another famous Nottingham company, Skinner and Rook Ltd, whose shop was on the corner of Clumber Street.

Shipstone's dray horses were a familiar sight around Nottingham for many years, delivering their loads of beer. This pair of white horses and their white-coated attendants have paused outside the Council House in the centre of Nottingham.

Hole's Brewery at Newark, with a more up-to-date delivery fleet. James Hole and Co. Ltd operated from the Castle Brewery on Albert Street, Newark, until they were taken over by Courage Brewery in 1967.

Lady tram conductor. The advent of the First World War depleted the ranks of men available for work and the first female conductor was employed on the Nottingham system in October 1915. Although in Glasgow women were engaged as tram drivers it was not thought a desirable step to take in Nottingham.

Resplendent in top hat and dress coat with decorative buttonhole, this is the driver of Bamforth's horse-drawn bus. This service ran from St Peter's Square, Nottingham, to Musters Road, West Bridgford, until

1912. This was a good job in pleasant weather, but open to the elements in inclement weather it must have been very uncomfortable.

Bus driver and conductor, Wollaton Street, *c.* 1927. Buses of the mechanized variety required both a driver in the cab and a conductor in the main body of the bus. This fine example, with outside stairs, operated between Nottingham and Bulwell/Hucknall.

Bus mechanics. Fondly remembered by many, trolley buses ran in Nottingham from 1927 to 1966. The last trolley bus in Nottingham, no. 506, is seen here ignobly being hitched up to a tow truck for an assisted passage back to the depot.

A sadly disappearing species: the garage forecourt attendant, who would fill your vehicle with petrol. Ward's Garage was situated in Daybrook and sold both BP and Shell. Inside, a pair of fine cars stand ready for sale.

Clifford's Motories in Eastwood, motor cycle retailers, 1913. On the back of this postcard the company offered to supply any make of motor cycle bar Triumphs at £4 off list price, which in those days, just before the First World War, was a bargain.

St Peter's Church, Nottingham, November 1965. The bells had been sent away to be recast. Here, the delicate task of unloading and rehanging the returned bells is being completed with the aid of a crane.

At the top of the railway hierarchy was the station master. Here is the one at Ollerton on the Great Central Line. The station is specially decorated in honour of the King in September 1908.

This postcard shows a pair of station porters waiting on an empty Sturton station (near Retford) for the arrival of a train, 1905.

The well-known *Little John* steam barge towing another craft along the River Trent, 1913. The river was a major thoroughfare for raw materials and manufactured goods.

Canal barge. Cropwell Bishop is on the Grantham canal and S. Heaselden operated his boat *Two Sisters* from the village. Coal and groceries were brought by canal from Nottingham and the local gypsum works once regularly used the canal to transport the gypsum to manufacturers.

Many boatyards, like this one at Lenton, sprang up to service the boats on the waterways. Keeping the boats and canals in good repair was essential, as many firms relied on water transport to move their goods.

The Lock, Holme Pierrepont. Nottinghamshire is criss-crossed by a number of canals that formed a major haulage system in earlier days. To facilitate going up and down hills locks were built. This Trent Navigation Company barge has tied up close to Holme Pierrepont Lock.

In the more rural areas at the beginning of this century, many roads were still in poor condition. Here Arthur Clay of Manor Farm, Kimberley, is spraying water from his cart on to the road in order to keep the dust down.

Just as roads needed maintaining so did the waterways. This Edwardian view shows a mud clearer operating on the River Trent near Sutton.

SERVICE INDUSTRIES

The post office at Edingley, near Southwell. In Edwardian times even the smaller villages had their own post offices, providing a service to the community and employment for locals. Here the post-boy can afford time out to lean on his bicycle and pose for the photographer.

PC 187 of the Nottingham force turned out in his best uniform in May 1913.

A policeman on Long Row, Nottingham, 1935. We still see policemen around but the sight of a policeman in a white coat in the middle of a main road directing traffic is very much a thing of the past. The famous Nottingham shop, Burtons, can be seen to the right.

Nottingham City Special Constables. The regular police force required its 'specials' in the early years of the century as now. A hat, a badge, and an armband together with some training, and this fine body of men was ready to do its bit.

NORMAN STREET.

The local doctor in Kimberley and Watnall was Dr Northwood, seen here being driven on his rounds by his groom, 1907.

Dr George Ross Northwood, like most professional men, was a pillar of the community, and it is not surprising that he was one of the first people in the area to own a car. Visiting his patients had become mechanized.

Nurses were never more urgently needed than during the world wars. Many women volunteered to help, often in temporary hospitals like this one at Eastwood. A significant number found it their vocation and stayed on after the wars.

The St John Ambulance Brigade has long given valiant service to the community. Photographer G.S. Ellis captured the Mansfield Division on film in 1916. It is interesting to note that they are all male.

The village schoolmasters at Kimberley British School, 1910. The schoolroom furniture is set out as normal for these times, with the desks all in rows facing the teacher. However, the large number of pictures and displays tend to suggest that this was some special occasion.

In 1908 Southwell's fire brigade consisted of eight men who served under Superintendent Robert Ellis. The primitive fire-engine was kept in a building on Queen Street. It could respond rapidly to an emergency in Southwell but would take longer to get to outlying villages.

Mansfield Waterworks, Rainworth. The area just to the north of Nottingham had several waterworks for pumping water to households and companies. Those at Papplewick and Newstead are best known today.

The gasworks, Sutton-in-Ashfield. These works, which were situated on Outram Street, were opened as early as 1852 providing a much-needed service to the town.

The lady window cleaners of Nottingham. The First World War saw changing roles for many, not least the female population, many of whom turned their hands to jobs unheard of pre-war. These ladies are shown on a postcard sent from Nottingham to Hednesford, Staffordshire, in June 1916. They appear to have a selection of ladders which they wheeled around Nottingham on the cart in the foreground.

The River Trent is a major obstacle to movement between the two halves of Nottinghamshire. A number of ferries plied their trade across the Trent: this one was at Farndon near Newark where, for a few coppers, you could be rowed across the river.

Waitresses in the Refectory, University College, Nottingham. The students at the newly opened College buildings at Highfields sat down to waitress service. In 1928 it was hard work for the waitresses, who served four rows of tables, with each row containing 144 places.

MISCELLANY

A billboard walker in High Road, Beeston. One of the more unusual jobs must have been to tramp up and down streets between boards festooned with advertisements. It is the simple unskilled jobs like this that have long since disappeared.

The demolition of old buildings has been taking place in central Nottingham for many years, often in the face of opposition from concerned groups. In June 1966 the Elim Temple, Halifax Place, The Lace Market, was knocked down.

The demolition of the slum area of Nottingham, known as Narrow Marsh, took place in the 1930s and provided a rich source of reclaimed timber. The auctioneer, wearing a trilby, on the right with his board, can be seen selling lots to a crowd of bargain hunters.

After demolition it is nice to see builders at work, as here at Kelham Hall in the 1920s. The Society of the Sacred Mission was extending the Victorian Hall to provide increased accommodation for the expanding Order.

The members of the Society of Sacred Mission at Kelham were not averse to physical labour themselves, and are seen here at work in their carpentry shop.

The monks at Kelham Hall. Although their life was quite a strict one, the monks did have the benefit of carrying out their calling in the ornate surroundings of Kelham Hall.

In the age of steam it was many a boy's ambition to be a train driver or fireman. Here is a scaled down version in the grounds of Thoresby Hall on which people could sit and dream.

The laundry at Daybrook has been a feature for many years, though few will remember it in the form shown here.

These itinerant basket workers were working in Basford before the First World War. The postcard tells us that the 'boss' is seated at the back and that they have just completed their contract, but are hoping for more work soon.

Many people were, and are, employed in shop work. The staff of the Maypole shop in Mansfield have lined up outside their store in May 1912. What the clown is doing as part of the group is unclear.

An Edwardian postcard published by Albert Hindley of Clumber Street, Nottingham, showing a man engaged in eel fishing on the River Trent at Colwick.

Will Temple's Burnt Cork Comedians. Without the modern standby of television people were more receptive to other forms of entertainment. Concert party shows were a feature of Nottingham life for many years. Will Temple, Entertainment Contractor, was based at 9 Wilford Grove, Nottingham.

ACKNOWLEDGEMENTS

Thanks are due to the staff of Nottingham Local Studies Library, in particular Joan Bray and Dorothy Ritchie, who are always on hand to give support and encouragement; also to Mr Adrian Henstock and the Nottingham Archives Department.

In addition I would like to thank those who so willingly made photographs available or gave permission to publish: those mentioned above, and also in particular Imperial Tobacco Ltd, Raleigh Industries Ltd, Plessey Communication Ltd, Scottish & Newcastle Breweries and M.W. Spick.

Attempts have been made to contact all copyright holders to obtain permission to use their material. If any have been unintentionally missed out I apologize.